The Children's Guide to...
PARIS

**Irma Kurtz
Clive Unger-Hamilton**

Illustrated by
Chris Winn

Travel Editor
Robin Staniforth

Blackie

Text copyright © 1984 Clive Unger-Hamilton/Irma Kurtz
Illustrations copyright © 1984 Chris Winn
First published 1984 by Blackie & Son Limited
Design by Robert B. McNab

All rights reserved

British Library Cataloguing in Publication Data
Kurtz, Irma
　　The Children's Guide to Paris
　　1. Paris (France)—Description
　　—Guide-books—
　　Juvenile literature
　　1. Title II. Unger-Hamilton,
　　Clive
　　914.4'3604838
　　DC 708

　　ISBN 0–200–72860–1

Blackie and Son Limited
Furnival House,
14–18 High Holborn,
LONDON,
WC1V 6BX

Printed in Great Britain by
Thomson Litho Ltd, East Kilbride, Scotland

Contents

I THE FACTS
How Paris Grew	7
The People	11
How the Government Works	13
Festivals and Holidays	14
The Language	15
Getting Your Bearings	16
The Métro	17
The Autobus	21
Taxis	22
Crossing the Road	22
Money	23
Conveniences	24
Taking Photographs	25
Writing Home	25
What to Take	26

II THE SIGHTS
The Eiffel Tower	28
Notre-Dame Cathedral	29
The Louvre	32
The Pompidou Centre	34
Arc de Triomphe	36
La Sainte-Chapelle	37
Jeu de Paume	38
Montmartre	39
Place de la Concorde	41
Les Invalides	42
Musée de l'Armée	42
Place Vendôme	43
Musée de Cluny	44
Les Tuileries	45
Place des Vosges	46

Musée de la Poste	47
The Quays	48
Palais Royal	48
The Catacombs	49
The Sewers	50
La Conciergerie	50
Musée de l'Affiche	51
Musée Rodin	52
Jardin des Plantes	53
Panthéon	54
Palais de la Decouverte	54
Musée de l'Homme	56
Musée de la Mode et du Costume	57
Musée Carnavalet	57
Bois de Boulogne	58
Musée de la Chasse	59
Musée de la Marine	60
L'Opéra	61
Montparnasse	62
Hôtel de Ville	63
Musée Grévin	63
Musée du Cinéma	64
Musée des Transports	64
Musée des Enfants	65
Aquarium du Trocadéro	66
Jardin du Luxembourg	66
Versailles	68

OFF-BEAT AND ODD

Royal Carp	69
The Rat Shop	70
Barges on Stilts	70
Motorised Poop Scoops	72

III WHAT'S ON
Finding out what's on   73

Boat Trips	74
Swimming	75
The Zoo	76

IV SHOPPING
The Big Stores	77
Shopping Suggestions	78

V FOOD AND DRINK
Restaurants and cafés	83
Picnics	89
On the hoof	89

EMERGENCY	90
INDEX	92, 93

Paris is special. Where else can you see the world's most famous picture, eat wild boar paté or wild strawberry ice cream, drink pomegranate milk, meet Napoleon's horse, stroll through the sewers or meet monster carp... all in little more than a few square miles?

You will find your own secret places in Paris, and your own favourite things to do. We'll show you around, help you with the money, explain the food, take you shopping and show you the sights. There are so many fine squares, churches, museums and restaurants to visit, as well as all the more bizarre places that help give Paris its unique, exciting atmosphere.

But you are the real explorer, and the memories you make will be your own. So—have a great time!

Yma and Cline

I
THE FACTS

How Paris Grew

Once upon a time, in the third century BC, a tribe called the Parisii lived on an island in the middle of the River Seine. It is the place now called the Ile de la Cité. Not only was this waterlocked land a natural stronghold, but it was also in the middle of the road that led from the Rhine to the Loire Valley. All traffic and commerce passed this way, and so the Parisii became prosperous. In 52 BC when Julius Caesar conquered them and the rest of France (then known as Gaul), he was especially impressed by the beauty and quality of the Parisii's gold coins. The Romans called the Parisii's homeland Lutetia. There are the remains of a Roman circus called the Arènes de Lutèce behind the Jardin des Plantes.

Soon Lutetia spilled over its island home onto what is today the Left Bank of Paris. In 507, King Clovis took back most of Gaul. He made Paris, as it was already known by that time, his capital. He drained the marshes and made the city much bigger. Clovis built a fortress where the Louvre now stands. Paris flourished, and by the middle ages it had become a famous centre of learning and of trade. Notre-Dame Cathedral and the Sainte-Chapelle date from this period.

In 1420, Paris fell to the English and in 1430 Henry VI was crowned there as King of France. Joan of Arc failed to get it back for France and was burned at the stake as a saint or a witch, depending upon which side judged her. In 1437, Charles VII recaptured Paris for the French. If he had not, the Champs Elysées might today be called the Elysian Fields and *you* might be eating snails for lunch.

By 1530, the royal family had a large and beautiful residence around the Louvre and the Tuileries. Paris had become more and more the centre for fashion and high society, but there was unrest too, and conflict between Catholics and Protestants. All through French history the Parisian crowd has been an important and dangerous element. It was partly to avoid the crowd, with their unpredictable temper, that King Louis XIV, "the Sun King", moved his court to a new palace at Versailles. To be frank, it was also because young Louis wanted to have fun with his friends where his mother and the rest of the older generation couldn't keep an eye on him.

In 1789, under the reign of King Louis XVI, the Parisian crowd grew desperate from hunger and heavy taxation, while watching their kings live in fantastic luxury. Revolution broke out. On July 14th, a mob stormed the Bastille Prison and released the inmates. In 1793, Louis XVI was executed by the guillotine. This decapitating machine was invented by Doctor Guillotin. It was supposed to provide a quick and painless end. (He experimented on sheep and presumably *they* told him it was quick and painless.) Thus began "The Terror" which lasted for nearly two years and sent more than 2,000 aristocrats to "The Nation's Razor", as the guillotine came to be known.

In 1800 the First Consul of the new French Republic, a remarkable man called Napoleon Bonaparte, managed to restore law and order to the troubled land. Napoleon was a very short man and there is one theory that it was to make up for his lack of stature that he became such a daring, ambitious soldier! Be that as it may, he was certainly able to imagine himself the ruler of France and maybe of the whole world. In 1804, he allowed himself to be crowned emperor in the Cathedral of Notre-Dame. In 1815, Napoleon was at last defeated at Waterloo by the Duke of Wellington, and he died in exile. While he ruled, he transformed Paris by building the Arc de Triomphe, the rue de Rivoli and the rue de la Paix.

Once again Paris became the home of a king, but this one had been installed by Napoleon's conquerors: the British and their allies. Parisians were still discontented and still hungry. There were more revolutions in 1830 and 1848. The Second Empire was then formed, with Louis Napoleon (the great Bonaparte's nephew) at its head. It was Louis Napoleon, or Emperor Napoleon III as he was proclaimed, who did more than anyone to create the lovely city you see now. He and his helper, Baron Haussmann, built sewers, bridges, railway stations, squares and wide boulevards. They swept away 30,000 old medieval houses and replaced them with the elegant façades which line the streets today.

In 1871 Paris fell to Germany after a long siege during which the population was so hungry they ate cats and rats. Even the animals in the city's zoo were slaughtered for food. After this, came another short and bloody revolution called the Paris Commune. Thirty thousand people were killed and many of the city's monuments were damaged or destroyed, such as the Tuileries Palace.

In 1889 the Eiffel Tower was built for a trade fair. It became one of Europe's most recognisable landmarks and for no reason anyone understands it was soon the very symbol of Paris! In 1900, the Church of Sacré-Coeur was built, which also transformed the Paris skyline. The same year, the first Métro line was opened.

Paris was threatened by the Germans during the First World War, but it remained safe. However, during the Second World War, the German army rolled under the Arc de Triomphe and down the Champs Elysées. Finally, in 1944, Paris was liberated.

Between 1944 and 1958, twenty-five different cabinets held power, which is almost two a year! The Parisian crowd was growing restless again. Charles de Gaulle, a celebrated French patriot, came out of retirement and helped save his country from possible civil war. He also started the big job of cleaning and restoring the beautiful monuments. In 1968 the Fifth Republic of France was shaken by student riots and by a wave of strikes. Once again, the Parisian crowd was angry! The next year, de Gaulle resigned and Georges Pompidou was elected President. It was after him that the latest gigantic monument of Paris was named: the Pompidou Centre. And what you think of *that*, you must decide for yourself when you see it.

The People

Parisians move fast and talk fast. They are impatient and quick-witted. Parisians take some getting used to.

Be polite to them, always call them *monsieur* (m'syer) and *madame* (ma-dam), always say please (*s'il vous plâit*—see-voo-play) and thank you (*merci*—mare-si) and maybe they will show you some of the charm they are world-famous for.

A typical Parisian block of flats is built around a

central courtyard, sometimes with shops and offices facing the street on the ground floor. The outer door is released by a buzzer or, in modern buildings, by tapping out a code known only to the residents. Inside the front door is the concierge's apartment. The concierge is a very important person in Parisian life. She probably has a cat, a dog, and a canary to keep her company while she devotes her attention to all the comings and goings of her building. She sorts the tenants' post, receives packages for them, waters their plants when they are away from home, and protects the house from strangers. She also holds stern opinions on their manner of living.

Few Parisians have gardens, so they spend a lot of time in their parks and open-air cafés. In the park, when the weather is fine, Parisians play boules, chess or card-games. The children still play with hoops, and sail miniature boats in the ponds. Parisian women are very well-dressed and most of them are excellent cooks. Traditional households still have their main meal at midday but Parisians are very industrious so more and more of them take shorter lunch-hours now, preferring a big evening meal.

In the month of August, Paris closes down. Everyone goes away on holiday. The Government has tried to change this habit but, as you know (if you read How Paris Grew!), the Parisian crowd doesn't change without a major revolution.

How the Government Works

General Charles de Gaulle established the current French constitution in 1958. It is called the Fifth Republic. At that time France faced yet again the threat of civil war and so de Gaulle created a more powerful role for the president, who happened to be himself. The President is elected by the people for seven years and he appoints the Prime Minister and other top people in the government. The President can declare a state of emergency and dissolve the parliament.

Parliament is made up of a lower house called the National Assembly, and an upper house called the Senate. They work roughly like the British House of Commons and House of Lords. The National Assembly can bring the government down, and the Senate works as a watch dog and advisor. The Senate meets in the Luxembourg Palace, and the National Assembly meets across the river from the Place de la Concorde in the Palais Bourbon. The President works in the Elysée Palace on the rue du Faubourg St Honoré. During the French Revolution it was a dance-hall. It is also where Napoleon finally abdicated after the Battle of Waterloo.

French political parties cover the spectrum from far left to extreme right. As a matter of fact, the terms "left" and "right" as we apply them to politics were first used in France at the time of the revolution in the eighteenth century. How that came about is interesting. The National Assembly sits in a semi-circular room. Since its earliest times, the people who loved the monarchy and wanted to keep things just as they were, sat on the right. Those who wanted to reform and change government always sat on the left. Those who believed in finding a middle way between the old-fashioned right and the reforming left sat in the centre. Nowadays, the Socialists and Communists sit on the left, and the Gaullist parties sit on the right.

Paris is part of a region called the Ile de France. The Mayor of Paris is elected by the 109 members of the municipal council who are in turn elected by the people of Paris. There is one council for each of the twenty areas into which Paris is divided. These areas are called *arrondissements* (ah-ron-deece-mon).

Festivals and Holidays

The French keep all the major religious holidays such as Christmas Day and Easter Monday. They also close shop for The Feast of the Assumption on August 15th, and for All Saints' Day on November 1st. New Year's Day is a holiday too. They have a few special festivals all their own: July 14th, for example, when there is dancing in the streets and fireworks to celebrate the storming of the Bastille Prison. Many places are closed on May 8th in memory of the end of the Second World War. On November 11th, there is a big, solemn military parade to celebrate **Armistice Day**. May 1st is **Labour Day** and a national holiday in France.

Most Parisians take their annual holiday in August and many shops and restaurants are closed then, but the museums are packed out with foreign tourists.

Most places are open on Saturday and closed on

Sunday, but each area of Paris has its own closing weekday. This weekly closing day is often a Monday. Note well that many monuments and museums are closed on Tuesday.

The Language

French is known as both the "language of love" and the "language of diplomacy", which, if you think about it, makes sense. It is amazing how much French you can learn in just two or three days if you keep your ears and eyes open, and if you're bold enough to open your mouth once in a while. Many of the words on shop signs and menus are the same as English, only they are pronounced differently. We have given you a rough and ready pronouncing guide for some French words. Do try them out. Parisians appreciate visitors making an effort to speak their language. Arm yourself with a little phrase-book before you visit Paris. Some of you might like to keep a vocabulary book and add words as you learn them. If you don't think this sounds like a fun-filled project, you might find it more amusing to work your way through one of the French comic-strip books like *Tintin* or *Astérix* with the help of a dictionary. The French call comic strips *bandes dessinées* (bon-dess-ee-nay) and are addicted to them.

If you ever find yourself in trouble, turn to your EMERGENCY section on page 90.

Here are a few basic expressions to be getting on with:

Ou est le... (oo-ay-ler...) = Where is the...

Combien s'il vous plâit? (com-byan-sill-voo-play?) = How much, please?
Excusez-moi (ex-skooz-aymwa) = Excuse me.

Getting Your Bearings

About three million people live in Paris and its suburbs, but the old city itself is small and its sights are fairly close together. The River Seine is the crucial landmark to hold in your mind. It makes a curve through the city and divides it into the Left Bank and Right Bank.

This division is more than just geographical. The Left Bank contains the famous Sorbonne University and was famous for a free, rebellious, slightly crazy approach to life. The Right Bank contains the workshops of the famous dress designers, the most expensive suburbs, the presidential palace, and the offices of big businesses. It is the home of the establishment and famous for high-fashion and conservative opinions.

The differences between the two banks of the Seine are not as great as they once were, but they still exist in the minds of Parisians. Two important islands lie in the middle of the Seine. You could say they are the heart of the city. The Ile de la Cité, which is the bud where Paris began centuries ago, and the Ile St Louis (eel-san-loo-ee). A footbridge connects these two. Locate them on your map and you will notice that most of the main sights are nearby.

The forty square miles of Paris are divided into 20 arrondissements, or districts, which are known by number: 1er (first), 2e (second), 3e (third) and so on.

Some of the streets in Paris are very long and cut through several arrondissements so it is important to know the district number you want, especially if you take a taxi. The best way to get around Paris is by underground. (See our section on THE METRO). Streets in Paris are called *rues* (roo). Avenues and boulevards are as in English. Before you set out to explore, please read CROSSING THE ROAD, page 22.

The Métro

There is no better way to get around Paris than on the Métro or, to give it its grand name, the Chemin de Fer Métropolitain. The Métro began in 1900, about 37 years after the London Underground. There are 353 stations, and as Paris is a relatively small city this means they are rather close to each other. Most Métro lines follow main streets. This is because they were not built by tunnelling but by digging up roads and then covering them over again. Some of the Métro stations still have the original entrances. They were made in a style of design called *art nouveau* (ar-noo-voh). This was a "look" popular at the turn of the century. You can recognise it by its flowing, sweeping curves and its use of tulip shapes. Many Métro stations have been modernised in a fanciful way. Be sure to look at the Louvre station which is decorated with copies of masterpieces from the great museum.

The Métro is easier to use than it is to explain. All lines have numbers, but hardly anyone bothers with them. What counts are the names at the opposite ends of the line. They are called *directions* (dee-reck-

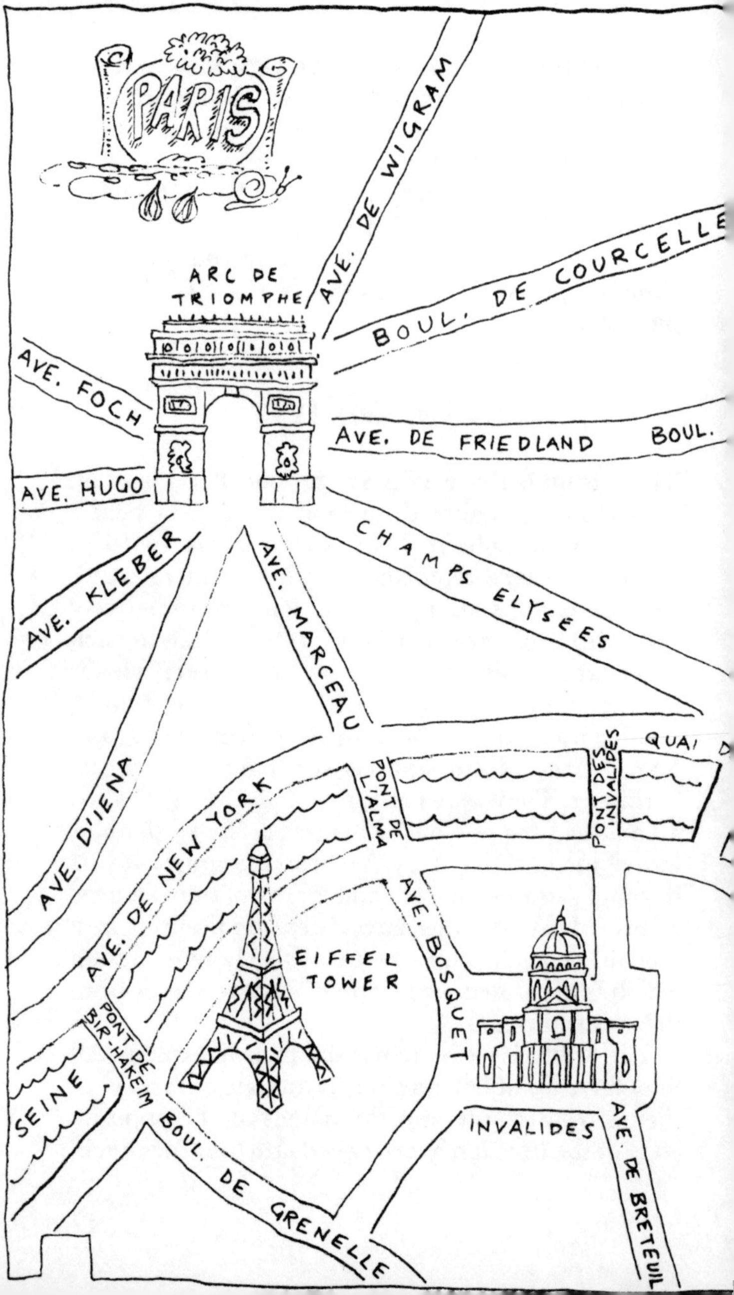
PARIS
AVE. DE WIGRAM
BOUL. DE COURCELLE
ARC DE TRIOMPHE
AVE. FOCH
AVE. DE FRIEDLAND
BOUL.
AVE. HUGO
AVE. KLEBER
AVE. MARCEAU
CHAMPS ELYSEES
QUAI
PONT DE L'ALMA
PONT DES INVALIDES
AVE. D'IENA
AVE. DE NEW YORK
AVE. BOSQUET
EIFFEL TOWER
PONT DE BIR-HAKEIM
SEINE
BOUL. DE GRENELLE
INVALIDES
AVE. DE BRETEUIL

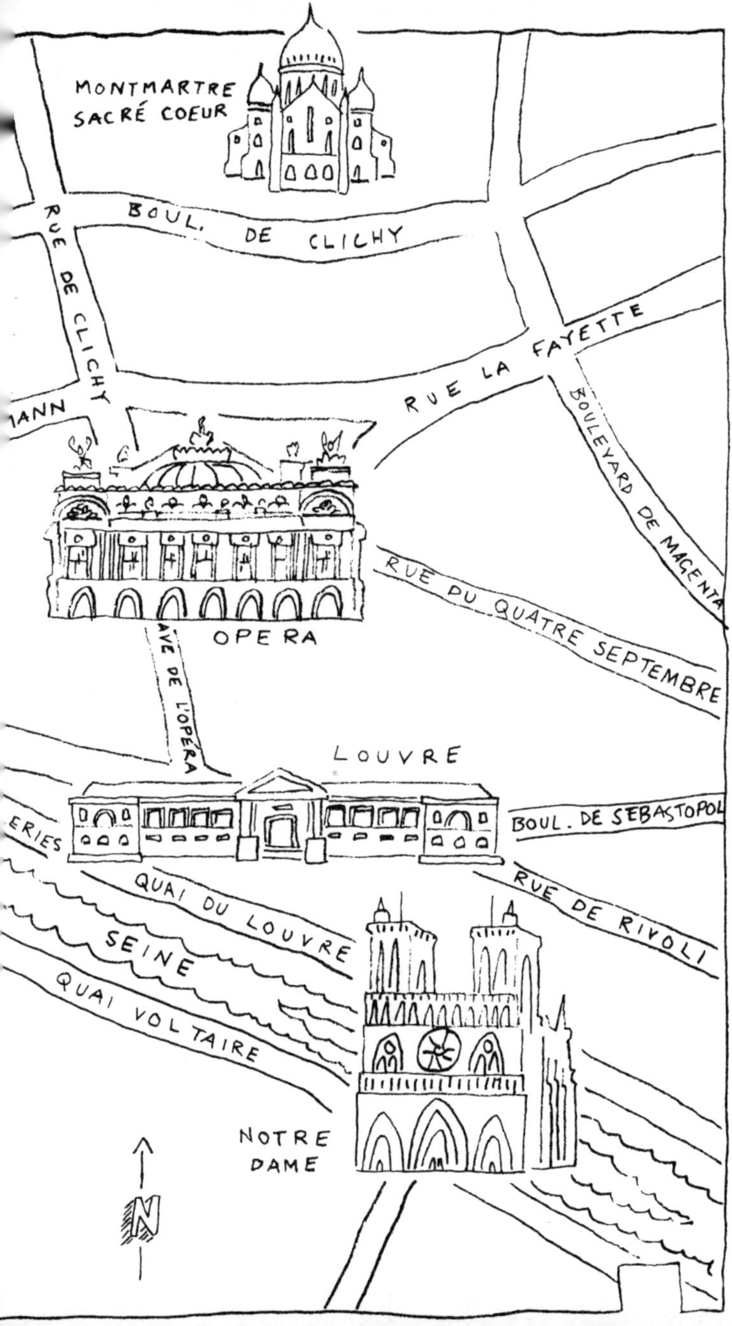

MONTMARTRE
SACRÉ COEUR
BOUL. DE CLICHY
RUE DE CLICHY
MANN
RUE LA FAYETTE
BOULEVARD DE MAGENTA
RUE DU QUATRE SEPTEMBRE
OPERA
AVE DE L'OPÉRA
LOUVRE
BOUL. DE SEBASTOPOL
ERIES
RUE DE RIVOLI
QUAI DU LOUVRE
SEINE
QUAI VOLTAIRE
NOTRE
DAME
N

see-on). If you want to go, let's say, from Concorde to Bastille (bass-tee), you take the line that ends at Vincennes (van-sen). In other words you will go in the direction of Vincennes. On the way back you go towards the opposite end of the same line, or in the direction of Neuilly (ner-ee). Of course, sometimes you will need to make a change to get to your destination. This is called a *correspondance* (core-eh-spon-dance). There are maps at every Métro station, and some of them have route-planners that are fun to use. Simply press the button next to your destination on a panel in front of the map, and your route will be illuminated in fairy lights.

Tickets (*billets*—bee-ay) are bought from booths in the station and then fed into an automatic turnstile. Collect your ticket at the other side of the turnstile and hold onto it in case an inspector boards your train. It will save money if you buy a packet of ten tickets (*un carnet*—uhn-car-nay). There is a first-class compartment at the middle of each train, but it is not worth the extra money.

You cannot get badly lost in Paris if you know the address of where you are staying, the nearest Métro, and if you always have a couple of Métro tickets in your pocket. Trains start at 5:30 am and stop around 1:15 am.

We must give you one serious warning to pass on to the rest of your party: over the past years the Métro has become infested with pickpockets. These villains are unusual because they are children, some of them less than ten years old. They work in gangs of three or four. Maybe they do look adorable, but don't let that fool you. They are skilled criminals. One will tug your sleeve or try to distract you in some way while his (or her) henchkid dips into your pocket. Watch out for them. Keep a tight hold on your wallet or handbag.

The Autobus

The Paris bus system is not as efficient as the Métro. However, if you are a good traveller you'll want to try everything at least once. The bus system is complicated. It helps if you speak a word or two of French. The same tickets are used as on the Métro, but you may need two of them for a long journey. Written along the outside of each bus is the route it runs. Make sure you are waiting on the right side of the street for the stop you want or you can be carried off in altogether the wrong direction. The bus-route is also written on a sign at each stop. Avoid using the bus during rush-hours. Parisians do not like to queue and there is a system of priority boarding which can end in violence. Most buses stop running at around 9 pm.

Taxis

The Parisian taxi driver is a character. He is known for smoking a cigarette without removing it from his mouth, for bad temper, for his salty sense of humour, and for not always taking tourists on the shortest route to their destinations. Taxis do not cruise as a rule but are found at regularly-spaced and numerous ranks called *Têtes de Station* (tet-duh-stahsee-on).

Crossing the Road

Parisian temperament really lets rip behind the wheel of a car. Street-crossing is a dangerous challenge for foreigners. In France, they drive fast, and they drive on the right. In theory, you look to your left when street crossing. However, many of the streets are one-way, or have extra bus lanes, so use your concentration and common sense, and *always* look both ways several times. Never rely on zebra crossings. Parisian drivers cannot be trusted to stop for pedestrians except at red traffic lights, and it's worth the trouble of walking a few blocks extra to find one. Some of the more terrifying boulevards have pedestrian subways. The worst crossing place in Paris (or Europe? Or the world? Or the UNIVERSE?) is over to the middle of the Place de la Concorde. Be ready to sprint—if possible a large group of you at the same time!

Money

The French unit of money is the franc (fronk). It is divided into 100 centimes (son-teem). The value of the franc varies all the time. At the beginning of 1984 there were just under 12 francs to the pound. This means one franc was worth a little over 8p. The banknotes in France are very beautiful. Study them while you have them. They don't last long. The coins can be confusing so try to get them straight before you start to spend them. There are coppery brown coins for 1, 2, 5, 10 and 20 centimes. There are silver coins for 50 centimes and for 1, 2 and 5 francs. There is a heavy, smallish, coppery-gold 10 franc piece too. Notes are worth 10, 50, 100, 200 and 500 francs. There are two sorts of 100 franc notes, but everything is clearly marked, so just take your time when you spend your money.

Paris prices are curious. Some things are much less expensive than you would expect. Other things cost a lot. A ride on the Métro, for example, is cheaper than London's underground, but a coca-cola at a pavement café can be expensive. Having your picture taken in a booth at the Eiffel Tower will cost more than a good three-course lunch in a simple restaurant. Watch the prices carefully. Try not to blow everything on Day One.

The best value for foreign currency is found at a bank. Most of them open between 9:30 am and 4:30 pm, but hours vary. They close on Saturday and Sunday. Big hotels and shops give an inferior rate of exchange. At weekends or on bank holidays you will find *Bureaux de change* (burr-oh-duh-shanje) at the major railway stations.

Conveniences

Ask for *la toilette* (lah-twa-let) or *le WC* (ler-doobluh-vay-say). Often these are unisex installations. The really primitive ones are no more than a hole-in-the-ground. When you see one of these, you will know it. You will also understand how it works. Many Parisian lavatories have a light that comes on automatically when you lock the door, *and not before*. Of course, in the posh hotels and restaurants the conveniences are deluxe. From the public WC to the Ladies (*dames*—dam) at the Ritz Hotel there is always a place to wash your hands. In big stations or squares you will probably find an attendant who expects you to leave 20 centimes in the begging bowl prominently displayed. Recently, modern free-standing cubicles have been installed in public places. They are oval in shape and built of ribbed concrete. Inside, music plays, and after each use they are cleaned mechanically, then squirted with perfume. To use them you must insert one franc in a slot outside.

Taking Photographs

It is satisfying to take your own photographs of

Paris, if you can. With a little care they can be just as good as postcards. Hunt around a bit for the best position. For instance, we think the Eiffel Tower is at its best when seen from the opposite bank of the river on the Avenue President Wilson. That way, you can include some houses in the foreground to give a better idea of the Tower's height. Notre-Dame, too, looks good from the opposite bank or even from behind.

Some of the museums allow photographs. The modern museums are light enough inside not to need a flash. If you do use flash, don't forget it won't work through windows or display cases. The light bounces from the glass and ruins your picture.

Best of all, is to take your camera when you are out for a stroll. Shop-windows, market stalls, the concierges with their fat little dogs, everyday scenes like these make the most vivid pictures and will capture your memory of Paris better than a million words. We're confident that you are too nice to take any snapshot that could embarrass or enrage the subject.

Film is expensive in Paris. Stock up before you set out. If you can, buy film at the duty-free shop on the way over. Even though the modern baggage X-ray machine at the airport is said to be harmless, you may prefer to carry your film through and keep the camera empty.

Writing Home

Ordinary picture-postcards of the sights are available absolutely everywhere. You can find them at all the tobacconists (*tabacs*—tah-bak). Stamps are sold there too. It is fun to look out for something a little special, even if it means buying one to send and another to keep for yourself. Old black-and-white postcard views of Paris can be found at the open bookstalls along the Seine for around one franc. Or you might prefer to go for a card featuring Napoleon's hat and coat, or a carved figurehead from a ship that fought at Trafalgar, or a shrunken head, obtainable from the kiosks in museums.

If you want to write letters, there is good, inexpensive stationery on sale in the Prisunic and Monoprix Supermarkets.

In the souvenir shops on the rue de Rivoli there is an interesting line in novelty ballpoint pens. You can buy them shaped like the head of Napoleon, for instance, or General Charles de Gaulle.

What to Take

1. A comfortable pair of shoes. You're going to walk miles, and many Paris pavements are made of granite.
2. A pocket calculator for instant currency conversion.
3. A paperback book or an electronic game for long journeys and for long queues.
4. A phrase-book.
5. A penknife for picnics.
6. It isn't absolutely necessary, but you might like to have a small torch, a compass, and a plastic raincoat.
7. Your camera!

II
THE SIGHTS

Paris is full of museums, churches and monuments, and in the summer it is also full of tourists visiting them. In August you can go from one fascinating attraction to another in Paris without encountering a single Parisian, but only other foreigners from lands as distant as Russia, America, Japan and the countries of Africa. Remember, Paris *itself* is a tourist attraction. Look out for the special sights of everyday Parisian life. Watch for schoolchildren shaking hands on a street corner. And for cyclists manoeuvring traffic with long loaves of French bread in their delivery baskets. A few yards from the busy boulevards, discover cobblestoned streets where you might think the clocks had stopped two hundred years ago and more. Catch a glimpse of courtyards full of flowers and statues. Keep a sharp eye out for the river barges with the bargee's laundry hanging on the line. Don't miss the sleepy, fat Parisian cats curled up in the windows of shops. Listen to the sound of metal gratings being pulled back from store-fronts in the morning, and the racket of impatient traffic. Use your nose too! Sniff sugary summer smells and roasting chestnuts in the winter.

There are many specialised museums in Paris and you'll probably find one to suit your own interest. There are museums of dolls, stamps, locks, tapestries, and even tobacco! We can only tell you about a few of them here. We have included the nearest Métro station but not the prices of admission because these are always changing. The age for the reduced admission (*tarif reduit*—tah-reef-raid-wee) varies from place to place, and can even depend on the whim of the ticket-collector. Look as young as possible. We have started you out in this section with the most popular tourist attractions followed by some that are less well-known. Enjoy yourself!

The Eiffel Tower

The *Tour Eiffel* (tour-eff-ell) is the most famous landmark in Paris, and it isn't supposed to be there at all! It was designed as a showpiece for a trade fair in 1889 and it should have been dismantled afterwards. Somehow nobody had the heart to take it apart, and so it just stayed where it was. Now, it attracts more than one million visitors every year.

When the Eiffel Tower was constructed, it was the highest building in the world (984 feet or 300 metres) and it kept that record for more than forty years. It took three hundred steeplejacks three years to build the tower, and it used two-and-a-half million rivets. They say that to stop it rusting, a team of painters must start work at the bottom each year and that by the time they get to the top, they have to start all over again. (To be honest, you'll probably never see a painter at work on the Eiffel Tower, but it makes a nice story.)

The design was by Alexandre-Gustave Eiffel, and it is so sturdy that in even the strongest wind, the top sways no more than $4\frac{1}{2}$ inches. On a hot summer day, the tower is actually six inches higher than in winter.

That is because seven-thousand tons of metal struts expand in the heat.

The view from the top is stunning. On a clear day you can see for more than 40 miles. The first two stages of the tower can be climbed on foot which is cheaper than taking the lift and fun too, as long as you have a good head for heights. We do not recommend riding up the tower on horseback. A Russian officer did just that in the last century, and once is enough for that kind of thing.

Behind the Eiffel Tower you will see a flat, grassy area. It used to be a military parade-ground. The big building as its far end is the *École Militaire* (ay-cole-mill-ee-tare), which is the military school where the great army general, Napoleon Bonaparte, studied. He was admitted, by the way, because his examiners thought he would make a good *sailor*!

The Tour Eiffel is open from 10 am until late in the evening during the summer months. Between November and March it opens half-an-hour later. There are ice-cream and souvenir stalls to make the long queue bearable. On the riverbank below the tower there is a stall that sells good sausages and chips for about 15 francs.

Métro: Trocadéro. (You'll have to walk across the river.)

Notre-Dame Cathedral

Notre-Dame (not-red-am) is one of the finest and first examples in the world of what is called "gothic architecture". Gothic is a style the French created and brought nearly to perfection when they built this soaring, singing cathedral in 1163.

Gothic architects wanted their churches to look light and spiritual but at the same time to have solemn dignity. To make Notre-Dame appear almost to be floating on air, they used for the first time what came to be known as "the flying buttress". You will notice these supports running along the sides of the building, outstretched and free from the main walls. Don't they give an impression of flight and weightlessness?

When you stand back from the building, you can see that the lines of the architecture draw your eyes always upwards. If you are a religious person, you will have to feel you are raising your eyes towards God. This is what the architects intended you to feel. Inside Notre-Dame too, your eye cannot help but look up to where the sculpted columns stretch into the vaulting. While you are inside Notre-Dame, be sure to look at the stained glass windows. The round ones are called "rose windows" and we think they are particularly beautiful.

On the outside in the northwest corner is the entrance to one of the towers and to the belfry. If you have read *The Hunchback of Notre-Dame* or seen the film, you will be able to imagine Quasimodo swinging like a monkey from one rope to another. The view from the tower is in one way better than the one from the Eiffel Tower: because it is only 230 feet high, you can see everything going on below you. The square in front of Notre-Dame is the exact centre of Paris, by the way, and all distances from the city are calculated from this spot. The fantastic and hideous heads jutting out from the tower are called "gargoyles". These ugly fellows have the double job of scaring the devil away, and also draining rainwater through their open mouths.

There are some good shops outside the cathedral selling small souvenirs for a moderate price, and excellent postcards, some of them featuring the gargoyles. In the square, you might notice a little donkey pulling a cart full of sachets of lavender from Provence on sale for 15 francs. The donkey has a bucket strapped underneath him. No prize for guessing why.

The cathedral is always open, but please be careful not to disturb the religious service if it is going on. Some Sundays an excellent choir comes to sing. The organ is more than one hundred years old and has a mellow sound. In the treasury of Notre-Dame (*le trésor*—luh-tray-zor) there are holy relics, among them the Crown of Thorns and piece of the True

Cross, enshrined in sumptuous jewelled caskets.

The treasury is open from 10 am to 5 pm daily except Sundays.
The tower and belfry is open from 10 am to 5:45 pm in the summer and closes one hour earlier in winter. They are closed on Tuesdays.
Métro: Notre-Dame.

The Louvre

This is your chance to see the most famous painting in the world—the Mona Lisa. But there are more than five miles of galleries in the museum of the Louvre and they contain more than 400,000 works of art. So brace yourself!

In the foyer there is a stall selling many good guides in English. Choose one of them and decide what you want to look at before you start out. You can't possibly see it all! Maybe your party will want to ask at the information desk about one of the guided tours in English, but there is a thrill about making your own discoveries. Many of the amazing treasures in the Louvre were brought to Paris as the loot and plunder of victorious conquests. King Francis I, for example, brought priceless paintings back in the sixteenth century from Italy and Spain. The Egyptian collection was booty Napoleon claimed after his campaign in North Africa.

Everyone who visits the Louvre wants to see the Mona Lisa by Leonardo da Vinci. What makes this painting so very special is something nobody can explain. It's true that the artist was a genius and his technique was revolutionary when he painted it 500 years ago, but its colours are sombre and it is much smaller than you might have expected. Yet there is an undeniable charm about the lady's mysterious smile which continues to capture the hearts and imaginations of all who see it. The model was the wife of a rich Florentine called del Giacondo and that is why the French call the painting "La Joconde".

Unfortunately, there is always such a mass of tourists around the Mona Lisa you have to fight to get near her. A glaring safety glass has been put up in front of her too because a fanatic once tried to spray her with paint as a political protest. The armless statue of the Venus de Milo is another of the Louvre's superstars. Look for the two "Slaves" by Michelangelo with a charming little owl carved around the back of one of them. In the basement, don't miss the reconstruction of an Egyptian embalmer's workshop knows as "The Crypt of Osiris". A small torch is useful if you want to browse among the tombs in the bowels of the museum.

As you can imagine, there are masses of postcards, posters (25 francs and up), jigsaws and other souvenirs on sale in the museum. Beware of the overpriced junk being sold by pedlars outside the main entrance.

The Louvre is open every day except Tuesdays from 9:45 am to 5 pm. It is free on Sunday, but packed out as a result.
Métro: Louvre.

The Pompidou Centre

Some Parisians think this space-age building must be the ugliest building in the world, and others think it is wonderful. Well, it certainly is different. It is a big, glass box with all its pipes on the outside and colour-coded according to whether they are carrying water, electricity, gas or fresh air. Its architects (one of whom was English) wanted to create something eye-catching, and they succeeded spectacularly.

It is five storeys high and you can go from level to level on escalators that run *outside* the building in glass tubes.

The Centre contains all kinds of displays, films and exhibitions. On its third and fourth floors is one of the biggest collections of modern art in the world and some of the craziest, wittiest pictures and sculptures ever made. There is one exhibit with arms and legs bursting out of the walls. There is an incredible optical illusion room too. Everyone has to remove his shoes to go inside which makes it a bit smelly... but interesting.

President Georges Pompidou succeeded General de Gaulle and the Centre is named after him. There's an odd picture of him on a sort of venetian blind hung sideways just inside the main door. On the fifth floor of the Centre is a very good self-service restaurant, and on the ground floor is an excellent shop for cards and posters.

Outside, on the right of the building you will see a brightly-coloured fountain with lots of mechanical devices clicking, whirring and spinning inside. In the square next to the Centre there is always a carnival of street artists, buskers, clowns, fire-eaters, escapologists and all sorts of exotic performers. The French are world-famous for their mastery of the art of mime and if you are lucky you will see some mimers in the square, looking so much like clockwork robots you'd hardly think they were human.

The Pompidou Centre, known locally as the "Beaubourg" (bow-boor), is open from noon until 10 pm, but it is closed on Tuesdays. It opens two hours earlier on weekends.
Métro: Rambuteau.

Arc de Triomphe

This gigantic monument to French patriotism sits in the middle of the *Etoile* (ate-wal) which means "star" and is so called because twelve avenues radiate from it.

The *Arc de Triomphe* was commissioned by Napoleon in 1804 shortly after he became Emperor, but he died in exile before it was completed. In 1840, his body was disinterred from its lonely grave and a chariot carried his coffin underneath the arch and between vast crowds in the *Champs Elysées* to its final resting place in *Les Invalides*. The scenes sculpted on the sides of the arch show Napoleon's greatest victories.

The victorious allied armies marched through the arch after the First World War in 1919. Soon afterwards an unknown soldier was buried there and an eternal flame of remembrance set alight by his tomb. In 1940, Hitler's occupying armies marched under the great symbol of victory, and four years later General de Gaulle and the allies liberated the city so it was their turn to make the triumphal procession. About seventy years ago a group of daredevil pilots actually flew through the arch. More recently a man was fined heavily for "insulting the memory of French patriots" when he fried an egg over the eternal flame.

Two-thirds of the way up the *Arc de Triomphe* is a small and rather boring museum, but the view from the top is terrific. There are telescopes (2 francs) through which you can study the fine art of Parisian driving. Because of the French system of priority to the right, all drivers on all twelve boulevards approaching the *Etoile* have right of way. It is a little miracle any of them survives to drive another day. Don't even think about crossing the road. Use the subway at the corner of the Champs Elysées. Children may climb the arch free of charge.

The *Arc de Triomphe* is open every day except Tuesday from 10 am to 5 pm. One hour earlier in winter. Métro: Etoile.

La Sainte-Chapelle

When you look around this magical building it seems to have no walls at all to speak of, but just an expanse of sparkling stained glass. There are fifteen windows, fifty feet high, extending over nearly 7,000 square feet. And they are more than 700 years old!

The Sainte-Chapelle (sant-sha-pell) was built by King Louis IX in the middle of the thirteenth century to house the Crown of Thorns. It was a miracle of Gothic architecture, and it still is. The building is on two floors and the part to see is upstairs. Stand at the back of the chapel and look to your left as you face the altar. The windows begin by depicting Genesis and they go on to show more than 1,000 stories from the bible. Try to visit on a sunny day when the colours glow like cut jewels.

The Sainte-Chapelle is inside the Palais de Justice. Its entrance is on the Boulevard du Palais.
Open from 10 to 11:45 am and 1:30 to 5 pm (one hour earlier in winter). Closed on Tuesdays.
Métro: Cité.

Jeu de Paume

The French invented the game of tennis and it was in this very place it used to be played in its original version. It was then called the "game of the palm" or, in French "jeu de paume" (jer-der-pome).

Now, the Jeu de Paume houses the finest collection of Impressionist paintings in the world. Oddly enough, these paintings were denied a showing by the major official art exhibition (it was called the "Salon") of their own time. About one hundred years ago when the works now so proudly displayed at the Jeu de Paume were first painted, all the critics laughed at them. The name "Impressionists" was given to the artists as a joke, because it was thought that unlike the solid work of the older painters with their classical and biblical themes, the new fellows represented only a fleeting "impression" of a moment.

You can see for yourself that these revolutionary artists did not draw hard lines in the classical, old-fashioned way but they painted light itself in dabs and particles of pure colour. The most famous of them were Monet, Manet, Pissarro, and Renoir. Many other famous artists of the time, such as Van Gogh, Gauguin, Toulouse Lautrec and Seurat were very influenced by the school of Impressionism. Just relax and let the airy magic work on your eye. Unlike the critics of their own time, you will be impressed by the Impressionists.

The Jeu de Paume is on the corner of the Tuileries gardens and the Place de la Concorde.
It's open from 9:45 am to 5 pm but closed on Tuesdays.
Métro: Concorde.

Montmartre

At the turn of the century, Montmartre (mon-mar-trer) was the artistic centre of France and, indeed, of Europe. Van Gogh, Manet, Modigliani, Toulouse Lautrec and many other great artists were drawn to this area of the city. The lifestyle of the artists here was so free and easy that it shocked the proper citizens of Paris, just as some people nowadays have been shocked by punk. The artistic crowd were called "bohemians" then, and where they lived on the steep hill of Montmartre there was a cheap and cheerful nightlife. These days, it isn't so cheap! However, the atmosphere of those romantic times is still to be found in the narrow, winding streets and cosy squares of Montmartre.

Start exploring from Sacré-Coeur Church, the beautiful white crown at the summit of the hill. You can get there on foot or by funicular railway. Just to the west of the church is Montmartre's most popular square, the Place du Tertre. There are lots of cafés here and some of them have jazz bands in the evening. It is also still full of artists but nowadays they offer to paint your portrait or to sell you one of their mass-produced pictures of Montmartre. Northwards on the rue des Saules you will come to Montmartre's own little vineyard. Just behind it is the *Musée de Montmartre* with its reminders of the old "bohemian" life of the area (open 2:30 to 5:30 pm). If you enjoy a good cemetery, visit the *Cimitière de Montmartre* where you can see the graves of many of the artists, writers and musicians who lived there.

To get to Montmartre take the Métro to Anvers, and walk up the hill or take the little railway.
The Church dome is open from 9 to 12 am, and from 2 to 5 pm. It has a fine view.

Place de la Concorde

There has never been anything very harmonious about the *Place de la Concorde* even though its name in English is the "Square of Harmony". In the eighteenth century the guillotine stood here. It was on this spot that Louis XVI was beheaded, followed by his wife, Marie-Antoinette. Over the next two years, more than one thousand people were guillotined in this square. In due course, those who condemned the royal family to death, such as the revolutionaries Danton and Robespierre, met their own cruel destiny under the blade of "Madame la Guillotine".

In the centre of the *Place de la Concorde* stands an Egyptian obelisk which is more than 3,000 years old and a twin to Cleopatra's Needle in London. The Concorde Bridge, which leads from the square across the Seine, was built after the great revolution with stones from the Bastille, so the people of Paris could trample on the walls of that grim prison. To the north, looking up the rue Royale, you will see the church of the Madeleine which was modelled on the Parthenon in Athens. It is balanced on the far side of the river by the columns of the National Assembly.

There is definitely nothing harmonious about the traffic in good old Harmony Square. See CROSSING THE ROAD and watch your step!

Métro: Concorde.

Les Invalides

After his defeat at Waterloo in 1815, Napoleon was banished to a small island in the South Atlantic called St Helena. He died there. His body was only allowed back to France in 1840 and, dressed in his favourite uniform, it now lies at the centre of the Invalides (an-vah-leed) Church.

The crypt has been opened to reveal his tomb. Though all the ornate marble decoration may not seem to be in the best of our modern taste, you cannot deny that it is very grand and befitting a great warrior. Inside a big, red porphyry casket there are six coffins—one of oak, one of ebony, two of lead, one of mahogany, the smallest of iron—and in the last one lies Napoleon.

Les Invalides and the buildings around it are a home for ex-servicemen rather like the Chelsea Pensioners' home in London. There is a military museum here too, called the Musée de l'Armée. It is best to visit the museum first because the same ticket will get you into the church free.

The Invalides Church is open daily from 10 to 6 pm (one hour earlier in winter).
Métro: Invalides. (There's a good self-service restaurant right near it.)

Musée de l'Armée

There is enough medieval equipment in this museum to fight a good-sized war. This is perhaps the best collection of its kind anywhere.

Model soldiers, suits of armour, uniforms, Renaissance swords, daggers, rapiers, muskets, blunderbusses and even the earliest guns of all which are called harquebuses are here to see. There are battle plans too. Among the more up-to-date war tools are the first tanks, which turned the tide in the trench warfare of the First World War and saved Paris from the German army.

See the actual bullet that killed the Vicomte de Turenne in 1875! And have a look at the wooden leg of another old hero, General Daumésnil. (He once said, "I'll retreat when the enemy give me back my leg!") There is Napoleon's famous grey coat and his famous black hat and, believe it or not, there is even the famous horse he took with him into exile. Don't bring sugar lumps. The horse is stuffed.

Allow plenty of time for this musuem. You can stock up on off-beat postcards at the souvenir stall, where you will also find packs of cards decorated with various uniforms.

The Museum is behind the big, domed church. It is open daily from 10 am to 6 pm (one hour earlier in winter.)
Métro: Les Invalides.

Place Vendôme

The Place Vendôme (plas-von-dom) is an elegant example of seventeenth-century French architecture. It now contains expensive shops and above them the lavish apartments of the rich and famous. In the middle of the square you will see a tall, bronze column made from twelve-hundred melted-down cannons. Napoleon's army captured them at the

Battle of Austerlitz in 1805. On top of the column is a statue of... guess who? He is wearing a military uniform now, but the original statue had him dressed in a Roman toga.

Set in the wall of No 11 on the square is the official standard for the length of the metre. It was defined by French scientists in 1791. Their calculations were all wrong, but they've stuck to the measure anyway.

On the first floor of No 12 is the flat where the composer Chopin died in 1849.

The Place Vendôme is between the rue de Rivoli and the Opéra.
Métro: Tuileries.

Musée de Cluny

Many of the museums in Paris are monuments in themselves. The Cluny Museum was established on the site of a fifteenth-century abbey. Much earlier, a Roman bath-house stood on this place. If you look through the railings from the Boulevard St Michel you can still see the ancient ruins.

The Cluny now houses arts and crafts of the Middle Ages. There are medieval clothes, tools and everyday utensils as well as jewellery, armour and wrought ironwork. Much of the work here comes from the dark days of plague and superstition. Maybe that is why there is a melancholy mood to the Cluny.

Nevertheless, a set of six beautiful tapestries called *The Lady and the Unicorn* series is so cheerful and bright with its rich colours and the delightful animals, flowers and leaves, that it must have seemed a promise of happy days to come to the people of long ago. Look out for a very gentle lion with a sweet and silly face. He's looking out for you!

The Musée de Cluny is open from 9:45 am to 12:30 pm and from 2 to 5:15 pm but is closed on Tuesdays. It is beside the crossroads of the Boulevard St Michel and the Boulevard St Germain.
Métro: St Michel.

Les Tuileries

You will find it hard to believe that until the middle of the sixteenth century the enchanting gardens of the Tuileries (twee-ler-ee) were a rubbish dump!

In those days the clay soil was used for making tiles which in French are called *tuiles* and so the gardens were named. The royal family built a palace on this spot and very soon the parks around it became a favourite strolling place for Parisians. The mob burned the palace down during the Commune of 1871, but the gardens remained.

Running the length of the gardens by the river's edge is a raised terrace that was once the playground of the royal children. Beneath it ran a secret passage to the Place de la Concorde. It was through there that King Louis-Philippe ran for his life and escaped his pursuers in the revolution of 1848.

Near the Louvre and off the rue de Rivoli is a big area devoted to the playing of boules. This is the best place in Paris to watch and learn the ins and outs of the game. You can bring your own set of boules and play too.

Nearby is a large pond where French people of all ages love to sail model boats. In the afternoons, you too can hire a model sailing boat there for about 5 francs for half-an-hour. A little further west is a puppet theatre with a show every Wednesday, Saturday and Sunday at 3 pm. Admission is around 6 francs. Behind this, are twenty lovely old wooden rocking-horses for toddlers. Watch how the stall-keepers time their rides. Good ice-cream and snacks are available here and it's a jolly place for a picnic.

On the outside wall in the rue de Rivoli at the Concorde end, you'll notice ten plaques surrounded by bullet holes. This is where ten French freedom fighters were executed by the Nazis in the Second World War.

Métro: Tuileries.

Place des Vosges

The Place des Vosges (plas-day-voje) is the oldest square in Paris and one of the most beautiful.

It is in the middle of an ancient quarter called Le

Marais (ler-mar-ay) which was once a marsh. The square hasn't changed much since the days when it was built for the royal family. Duels were fought in the gardens in the middle. Sit outside in a café and imagine what it was like in the seventeenth century when carriages arrived in the darkness before dawn, bringing men to these fatal encounters. Tucked away in a corner of the square is what must be the smallest shop in Paris. It sells antique clothes and jewellery. Victor Hugo, who wrote *The Hunchback of Notre-Dame*, used to live at No 6. His house is now a museum.

Métro: Bastille.

Musée de la Poste

If you collect stamps, you mustn't miss this fabulous postal museum. There is a collection of rare and famous stamps here as well as a really interesting explanation of how communications have evolved since the Middle Ages. There are exhibitions showing stamp printing machines and machines that sort the mail. Of course, there is also an excellent stamp shop.

The museum is at 34 Boulevard de Vaugirard. It is open daily from 10 am to 5 pm. Closed on Thursday. Métro: Odéon.

The Quays

The Quays along both banks of the Seine are lined

with bookstalls where you can buy old prints of Paris, antique cards and posters, maps, and—oh yes! books too! Mind you, the books are mostly in French.

On the right bank, a small animal market is to be found on the Quai (kay) de la Mégisserie. As well as the usual run of pets, you can buy a goose, a swan or even a peacock (they cost around £250). We have even seen a dwarf Vietnamese black pig here. Vietnam was once a French colony and Paris has a large Vietnamese population.

On the banks of the Ile de la Cité there is a vast, covered market where flowers are sold except on Sundays when it is converted to a bird market. If you are lucky enough to be invited to a Parisian home for dinner, it is customary to take flowers for your hostess.

Palais Royal

In the seventeenth century Cardinal Richelieu was one of the cleverest and most important men in France. King Louis XIII himself was obedient to this wily Minister who increased his own power by increasing the power of the throne. He was, in fact, the power behind the throne. It was he who built the immense palace called the Palais Royal.

Now, it is mostly state offices. On its west side is the celebrated French classical theatre called the Comédie-Française. Parisians use the garden in the courtyard as a park and meeting place. On the lawn in its centre is a miniature cannon that used to be fixed to fire every day at noon when the sun ignited the gunpowder inside it. This is a good spot for picnics. You might like to stroll around the shops. In one of them, young Charlotte Corday bought the very knife with which she stabbed the political extremist Jean Paul Marat as he sat in his bath.

The entrance to the Palais Royal courtyard is opposite the Palais Royal Métro and beyond a small forecourt of parked cars. The courtyard is a public throughway and is never closed.

The Catacombs

By the eighteenth and nineteenth centuries, the cemeteries of Paris were full to overflowing. Millions of bones had to be transported to a network of underground Roman stone quarries in the south of the city. These are called the catacombs (*Les Catacombes*—lay-cat-a-cormb).

A sign over the doorway tells you that "you are now entering the Kingdom of Death". Truer words were never written! Mountains of bones neatly sorted into skulls, ribs and lesser bits, lie on every side of the chambers and corridors. It is creepy, to say the least. During the Resistance when the Germans occupied Paris, brave freedom-fighters used the catacombs as their headquarters. Bring a torch with you, for the lighting is dim and grey. This is a good place to buy very unusual postcards.

You can visit them in the summer every Saturday at 2 pm, but from October to June, they are open to the public only on the first and third Saturday of each month.
Métro: Denfert-Rochereau.

The Sewers

Les Egouts (lays-ay-goo) or the Sewers, are one of the wonders of Paris.

Once you are under the surface, a long corridor which is dank and smelly leads to a display of pictures showing how this incredible network was built. Its tunnels follow Paris, street for street, like twisted subterranean shadows. There is an audio-visual show too, with free translating earphones. Weaker stomachs generally totter for the exits at this point.

The courageous can take a guided tour along some of the galleries. They are shown several places it would be a rotten idea to fall into. Watch your step. Some of the pathways are slippery and narrow. Colour views are on sale at the cash-desk but nothing can capture the smell!

The entrance is a trapdoor in the pavement on the Quai d'Orsay (kay-door-say) at the corner of the Pont d'Alma.
You can visit the sewers on most Monday, Wednesday and Friday afternoons between 2 and 5 pm. At holiday times, the queues for this rare treat are very long.
Métro: Alma Marceau.

La Conciergerie

A blade and a ladder from one of the first guillotines are on show at the Conciergerie (con-sea-air-jeree). This grim prison was the final home for many of the aristocrats, and it was the last thing they saw before a brief trial and the guillotine.

You can visit the little "barber's shop" where the prisoners' hair was cut short and their arms tied. Afterwards they were led straight out to the waiting wagons that carried them to their doom. Queen Marie-Antoinette spent the last months of her life in this dark, sad place. She left behind some pathetic mementoes that you will see here. Among them is a copy of a note she wrote by pricking holes in a scrap of paper because her jailors would not let her have a pen.

More than 2,500 prisoners passed through the Conciergerie on their way to execution. If ever a place was haunted by fear and misery, this one is!

The Conciergerie is open from 10 am to 12 noon and 1:30 to 5 pm (4 pm in winter), but it is closed on Tuesdays.
The entrance is on the Quai de l'Horloge.
Métro: Cité.

Musée de l'Affiche

The French pioneered the art of the poster in the nineteenth century. You might say they were the first advertising men. Maybe you've seen the beautiful ads for the Moulin Rouge and other Montmartre music halls designed by the famous Toulouse Lautrec, or Alphonse Mucha.

The Musée de l'Affiche (moo-zay-der-la-feesh) was opened in 1978 to house thousands of colourful posters advertising all kinds of products and performances. Copies of them are on sale. You are bound to find one that would make a perfect souvenir of Paris to have on your bedroom wall.

The Musée de l'Affiche is at 18 rue de Paradis.
It is open from noon until 6 pm, Wednesday to Sunday.
Métro: Gare de l'Est.

Musée Rodin

Auguste Rodin (ro-da) was a famous sculptor of the late nineteenth century. This museum is the actual house and garden where he worked in his old age.

There is a good chance you will recognise his famous statue of "The Thinker". He sits in Rodin's garden. What do you suppose this young man is thinking so seriously about? Maybe he is thinking about a way to come in out of the rain.

The Rodin Museum is in the Hôtel Biron in the rue

de Varenne.
It is open from 10 am to 12:15 pm and from 2 to 5 pm, but is closed on Tuesdays.
Métro: Invalides.

Jardin des Plantes

These are the botanical gardens of Paris, but the main attraction is the Natural History Museum and the zoo. Mind you, the zoo is rather small. It used to be very large but during the Prussian siege of Paris in 1871, the people were so hungry they ate the animals.

There is a children's section where you are allowed to touch the animals. You cannot touch the creatures in the Vivarium, however, which houses bats, toads and snakes. There is a mean Green Tree Viper from Cambodia. In its native land it hangs around in bunches of bananas and bites the labourers who come to gather the fruit. This is the reason for so many missing Cambodian fingers! The viper's bite is deadly and the fruit-pickers' only hope is to lop off the bitten area before its venom spreads.

The zoo and the museum are good value, but the aquarium is run-down and seedy.

There is a good snack bar selling, among the usual foods, "Barbe à papa" which is French for "Father's Beard" or what we call candy-floss; and twigs of liquorice root.

Just behind the Jardin des Plantes you will find the ancient Roman ruins of the Arènes de Lutèce.

Métro: Gare d'Austerlitz

Panthéon

Some of the most famous men of France are buried in this huge and gloomy building. There are philosophers such as Voltaire and Rousseau, the writers Victor Hugo and Emile Zola; there are statesmen and soldiers too at rest here.

One of the most interesting, and, in some ways bravest men buried here is Louis Braille. In 1812, when Louis was only three years old, he lost his sight totally. He did not despair, however, but invented an alphabet for the blind based on touch which is still used. It is called "braille". The imposing domed building of the Panthéon was completed just before the Revolution. It was originally a church.

The Panthéon is open daily from 10 am to 6 pm but it is closed Tuesdays.
Métro: Luxembourg.

Palais de la Découverte

Please don't yawn when we tell you this is the Science Museum of Paris. It is the most exciting museum of its kind you'll ever see.

There is an area devoted to each important division of natural science and technology. There is also a space exploration section with a piece of moon rock, and a big planetarium that has special shows. The displays and demonstrations are terrific, but what is best of all is that you are allowed to participate in real scientific experiments.

White-coated experts will work with you and help you discover for yourself how chemical reactions take place, how the internal combustion machine works, how the telephone works, how lasers operate, and why we see colours the way we do. Quite a few of them speak English and they will answer all your questions.

Even if you spend a whole day there you would not be bored for a moment. Wednesday is the day Parisian schoolchildren go, and there are special demonstrations.

The museum is inside the glass and metal Grand Palais. It was built for the World Fair in 1900, and it makes a perfect setting for the thrill of discovery. The postcards are great. You can buy beautiful bits of coloured minerals at the entrance. There is a café too. See it all. It is brilliant!

The Palais de la Découverte (Museum of Scientific Discovery, in English) is on the Avenue Franklin D. Roosevelt.

It's open from 10 am to 6 pm, but is closed on Mondays. Planetarium shows (admission extra) are at 2, 3:15 and 4:30 pm.
Métro: Champs Elysées Clemenceau.

Musée de l'Homme

Meet Australopithecus Africanus and others of your distant relatives here in the Museum of Mankind.

There's a range of skulls and bones to show how we developed from the apes, and there are costumes from all over the world to show what we developed into. The Samurai armour is awe-inspiring. It must have taken a day to put it on and even longer to take it off.

Primitive tools and weapons are on display too. There are those tall lumps of rocks called Menhirs that ancient man used to stick into the ground for no known reason. (Obélix in the *Astérix* books carries one around with him.)

Folk customs from all over the world are illustrated. A couple of Colombian corpses tied up with string are on show and some shrunken heads for a touch of the gruesome. It is a big museum on two floors, and good fun for browsing around in. You'll find a café, gift shop and card stall in the entrance-hall.

The Musée de l'Homme is in the Palais de Chaillot on the Place du Trocadéro.
It's open daily from 10 am to 6 pm, but closed on Tuesdays.
Métro: Trocadéro.

Musée de la Mode et du Costume

Paris has been the centre of style and fashion for centuries. Rich women all over the world still do not feel their wardrobe is complete without a few Parisian frocks. Every year there are lavish shows where the French designers present their new collection of women's clothing to a breathless audience. It is fitting that the city should have an excellent Fashion and Costume Museum.

Some of the garments you will see here date back over two hundred and fifty years. There are the first platform shoes from the eighteenth century, and the curious padding nineteenth-century women used to wear over their bottoms. They are called "bustles", and how a woman wearing one managed to sit down is a puzzle.

If you know how to sew or if you are interested in designing clothes someday, be sure to bring a pad and pencil so you can copy some of the designs.

The Musée de la Mode et du Costume is in the Palais Galliéra on the Avenue du Président Wilson.
Opening hours only Wednesday to Sunday from 10 am to 5:40 pm.
Métro: Iena.

Musée Carnavalet

The grand houses of France used to be called "Hôtels", because until quite recently the French word "hôtel" simply meant a big house or public building. Many of the "hôtels" of Paris were built in the quarter known as Le Marais, and one of the most beautiful of all was the "Hôtel Carnavalet".

This splendid building has become the official museum of the City of Paris. Whole rooms in it have been carefully restored to show how people used to live. There is a very interesting collection here of everyday bits and pieces from the past. There are painted shop signs, antique jewellery, fans, souvenirs from the Revolution, and even a pair of satin slippers that belonged to Marie-Antoinette.

The Carnavalet Museum is not particularly big, which in our opinion is generally a good thing.

Musée Carnavalet is open from 10 am to 5:30 pm daily except Mondays.
It is at 23, rue de Sevigne.
Métro: St Paul.

Bois de Boulogne

There is nowhere nicer in Paris for a picnic than the Bois de Boulogne. It is an enormous park on the west side of the city where the royal families of medieval times used to hunt wild boar, bears, deer and wolves.

The wild beasts (and their hunters) are long gone, but there is still a lot to see and do in this 2,000 acre expanse. There are lakes, ornamental gardens, museums, two racecourses and an artificial waterfall.

A miniature railway will take you from the Porte Maillot to the Jardin d'Acclimatation. The Jardin d'Acclimatation contains what is said to be the best amusement park in the whole of France. It has a miniature car track, mini golf, a bowling alley, a circus, a puppet theatre and a zoo. There is also a giant doll's house.

Next to the Jardin d'Acclimatation is the Musée National des Arts et Traditions Populaires—a folk-museum. Here you will see all the traditional crafts, games, customs and country cottages of France. There are lots of buttons to push on the exhibits.

In the summer you can rent bicycles near the Pavilion Royal. From October to April they are available only at weekends.

The Bois de Boulogne never closes, but it is not a safe place to wander around in after dark.
The Jardin d'Acclimatation is open daily from 9 am to 6:30 pm but closes at dusk in winter.
Métro: Porte Maillot.

Musée de la Chasse

The French are mad about hunting. As a matter of fact, quite near Paris they still hunt wild boar in the woods and there are lots of deer. Venison and wild boar paté are on the menus of many restaurants. When the French like something, they devote a museum to it; so, of course, they have a Hunting Museum.

This museum is probably the only one of its kind in the world. There are stuffed examples of their favourite game animals. The most impressive is a towering polar bear which greets you at the door. You will also see all sorts of weapons, from elephant and rhino guns to crossbows. There are some stunning animal paintings and souvenirs of big-game-hunting expeditions.

The Musée de la Chasse is at 6 rue des Archives in the Marais quarter.
It is open daily from 10 am to 6 pm. It closes one hour earlier from October to March and it is closed on Tuesdays.
Métro: Hôtel de Ville.

Musée de la Marine

The Maritime Museum is full of nautical curiosities from old-fashioned diving suits and big glass lighthouse reflectors to a fully equipped ship's bridge that you can walk about on.

Right near Napoleon's state barge is an amazing antique machine-cannon that used to fire twelve balls in rapid succession. There are more model ships than you can shake a stick at, if you enjoy shaking sticks at model ships. There are good postcards and some unusual souvenirs such as miniature anchors and bosuns' whistles on keyrings from about 30 francs. It is light enough to take photographs inside.

The Maritime Museum is in the Palais de Chaillot beside the Trocadéro Square.
It is open from 10 am to 6 pm, but closed on Tuesdays.
Métro: Trocadéro.

L'Opéra

Picture a wedding-cake wearing a green hat and you'll know what the Paris opera-house looks like.

It took thirteen years to build and was opened in 1875. Even though in area it is the biggest theatre in the world, it only seats as many people as a good-sized cinema.

Most of its space is taken up by grand staircases and foyers. This is because it was built to reflect the imperial glory of Napoleon III. There was even a ramp built up one side of the building so he could step straight from his carriage into his seat in the auditorium. After all that trouble, he went into exile in England four years before the opera-house was finished. He was a keen opera-lover, but he never once got to hear an opera there.

There are guided tours of the Opéra and a little

museum of operatic mementoes. And there are sumptuous chocolates on sale there, too.

The Opéra is open from 11 am to 3:30 pm daily, but it is closed on Mondays.
Métro: Opéra.

Montparnasse

The ancient Greeks believed the gods and the muses of poetry and music lived on a sacred hill called Mount Parnassus. When this quarter in the southern part of Paris became the haunt of writers, artists and musicians it started to be known half-jokingly as Montparnasse, or Mount Parnassus. The joke stuck.

After the Second World War, Montparnasse (mon-parn-ass) replaced Montmartre as the artistic centre of Paris. Cafés and restaurants here were frequented by people like Stravinsky, Picasso, Scott Fitzgerald, Jean-Paul Sartre, and even Lenin. A café called *La Coupole* used to be the favourite haunt of the artists. It has now become the favourite haunt of the tourists looking for the artists. It still has its original decor and its waiters wear traditional white aprons.

The most dramatic addition to the quarter in recent years is the Maine-Montparnasse Tower, which at 688 ft, is Europe's tallest skyscraper. It is reckoned to have the fastest lift in Europe too. There is a café and restaurant at its top with a spectacular view, particularly at night when the city is lit up.

You can take the lift in the skyscraper daily from 9:30 am to 11:30 pm. Winter: 10 am to 10 pm.
Métro: Montparnasse-Bienvenue.

Hôtel de Ville

Don't try to book in here for bed and breakfast. "Hôtel de Ville" (oh-tell-der-vee) means "Town Hall" in French.

This is a nineteenth-century copy of an older building which was burned down by the mob in the revolution of the Paris Commune in 1871. The square outside it was for centuries the place where public executions took place. One of the guillotines was busy here during the French Revolution.

There was bloody street fighting on this spot in August 1944 when the German troops were being driven out of occupied Paris.

Métro: Hôtel de Ville.

Musée Grévin

The French have been making waxwork figures since the eighteenth century. Madame Tussaud set up shop in London when she fled from Paris after the Revolution. Some of the figures in the Musée Grévin (moo-zay-gray-vuh) look pretty dusty now but it remains an impressive collection of waxworks.

Upstairs, there is a special hexagonal room called the Palais des Miracles lined with distorting mirrors and fantastic columns. A beautiful old-fashioned light show is put on here. Next door is a little Victorian Theatre called the Cabinet Fantastique, where conjuring shows are given. The Museum opened just over 100 years ago and it has changed very little inside. It has a sweet, faded, old-world atmosphere to it. See it if you can!

The Musée Grévin is at No 10 Boulevard Montmartre.
It is open from 2 pm to 7 pm, and 1 pm to 8 pm on Sundays.
Métro: Richelieu-Drouot.

Musée du Cinéma

Another first for the French was the world's first ever moving-picture show. It was put on in 1895 by the brothers Louis and Auguste Lumière. You can see some of the earliest equipment in this Museum of Cinema as well as film-sets and costumes. The tour is rather long and it's in French.

There is a Museum of French Monuments upstairs if that's more to your taste!

The Musée du Cinéma is in the Palais de Chaillot (shy-oh) at the Trocadéro.
Tours start at 10 and 11 am and at 2, 3, 4 pm. It is closed on Mondays.
Métro: Trocadéro.

Musée des Transports

Wouldn't it be great to go back three hundred years and ride around Paris in a *fiacre*!

The *fiacres* were horse-drawn carriages that circulated the city charging passengers fares of a few pennies, or "sols" as the French currency was then. They made up the city's first public transport system. You can see them and all sorts of other vehicles at the Transport Museum.

Some of the old carriages were magnificently carved and christened with pretty names. There were *Gazelles*, for instance, and *Hirondelles* (swallows), and *Dames Réunies* (ladies joined together). The earliest trams, trolleys, buses and Métro cars look a lot more fun than the new ones.

The Transport Museum is near the Zoo at 60 Avenue Sainte-Marie.
It opens only on Saturdays and Sundays from 2:30 to 6 pm between April 15th and October 31st.
Métro: Porte Dorée

Musée des Enfants

If you think you have troubles, just imagine what it must have been like to be a child hundreds of years ago in Paris during the Revolution or before the First World War! At this fascinating Museum of Childhood you can see the horrid Little Lord Fauntleroy suits and the ghastly Miss Muffet dresses children had to wear in the last century. You can also see what poor, deprived boys and girls used to play with before the video-game and television were invented. There are some interesting models and gorgeous dolls here too.

The Musée des Enfants is inside the enormous Palais de Tokyo, built for the World Exhibition in 1937.
It is open from 10 am to 5:40 pm, but it is closed on Mondays.
Métro: Alma Marceau.

Aquarium du Trocadéro

The main attraction at this aquarium, as far as we are concerned, are the piranha fish. Just look at those teeth! One at a time, they aren't so bad but they travel in a school that is capable of eating the flesh off the bones of a big animal in a matter of minutes. Fortunately, they stick to South American rivers and European Aquaria.

Some of the fish in this small aquarium look good enough to eat, but others, like the Moray eel, look as though *they'd* like to eat *you*!

The aquarium is underground and built to resemble a grotto. It's fun and pretty cheap. There is a snack-bar outside and it's a good place to picnic.

The Aquarium du Trocadéro is in the gardens between the Palais de Chaillot and the river.
It is open daily from 10 am to 5:30 pm.
Métro: Trocadéro.

Jardin du Luxembourg

The Luxembourg Garden is a good place to stop,

rest and picnic. It is in the centre of a lot of tourist attractions near the Left Bank. Its tree-lined walks are soothing when you start to feel a little frazzled.

There are statues and fountains and a pool where you can usually hire a model boat to sail. Most afternoons there is a puppet show in a little theatre near the pool. You can buy an old-fashioned hoop at some of the kiosks in the Luxembourg.

The Parisians use this park a lot. You can see them playing boules, chess and cards. There are smart nannies taking smart babies for their afternoon walks.

Next to the garden is the Palais du Luxembourg where the Senate sits. Some of the old state apartments are open on Sundays between 9:30–11 am and 2:30–3:30 pm.

Versailles

Versailles was the most magnificent Palace in Europe when it was built for Louis XIV ("The Sun King", 1638–1715).

The inside of the Palace is splendid, particularly the Hall of Mirrors where, on 28th June 1919, the Germans signed the famous Versailles Treaty, ending the First World War.

But choose a fine day to see Versailles because the classical French gardens, which extend over 25 acres, are really worth a visit. The fountains or Grandes Eaux (gron-so) are spectacular too, but only working at certain times, so it's worth checking before you go. The Petit Trianon and the Grand Trianon, two miniature Palaces made of marble, can be reached from the far end of the 'Grand Canal' (part of the cross-shaped lake) or straight along the Avenue de Trianon from the Palace. Le Hameau (le-ammo, the hamlet), just across The Big Lake, is where Louis XVI's wife, Marie Antoinette, amused herself playing the "rustic". She used to dress as a shepherdess and had a country village built in her back garden, complete with thatched cottages around a duck pond, and a few shampooed and perfumed sheep to complete the scene.

Many stately, stylised (and very long!) operas, popular in the eighteenth century, were staged at the open-air theatre constructed in 1786 by Gabriel. The walls are hung with thousands of little stones, each one wired separately to its fastening to resonate and give better outdoor acoustics.

You can get to Versailles from Gare Montparnasse (there's even a double-decker train!) or you could take a coach or guided tour.

OFF-BEAT AND ODD

Royal Carp

There is an ornamental pond at the Place de la Concorde end of the Tuileries garden, and in it lives a family of carp said to have been there for over one hundred years. If you throw a bit of bread on the water, there is likely to be an almighty stir and swirling as the enormous fishes rise up to get it.

In the seventeenth century, the royal doctor to King Louis XIV was called Monsieur de l'Orme. He was inspired by carp just like these to a novel (not to say distinctly "fishy") theory.

Monsieur de l'Orme had noticed that carp lived to a great age, and he decided that must be because they make their home in water where there are neither winds nor draughts. To test his theory, he designed a set of special air-tight clothes for himself. He always wore six pairs of socks, and when he went out he put on several fur hats. Furthermore, he slept in a special heated closet surrounded by hot-water bottles, and to be on the safe side he always kept a clove of garlic in his mouth. You probably think Monsieur de l'Orme was pretty silly. But it has to be said that he lived to be nearly a hundred!

The Rat Shop

The area around the Pompidou Centre used to be a vast, all-night food market called Les Halles (lay-al). Not long ago, the market was moved out of the city to a site near Orly Airport. When the market flourished inside Paris it was a gourmet's paradise for rats. Indeed, rats were a problem in those days, and had been in Paris since the great plagues of the Middle Ages.

When you are strolling around the interesting quarter where the market used to be, have a look at No 8 rue des Halles. There you will see a shop that remains from the old rat-infested days. We call it the Rat Shop. The sign over its door says *Destruction des Animaux Nuisibles* which means, roughly: Vermin Extermination. The windows of the shop are a riot of stuffed rats, rather moth-eaten, and the methods of doing them in! If you like that sort of thing it's worth a photograph.

Barges on Stilts

The Seine is a busy waterway and in constant use. Apart from all the tourist boats, there are big barges continually passing up and down. Some of these barges are so wide they fit between the arches of the bridges with only a couple of feet to spare.

To help the helmsman steer safely under the bridges, the wheelhouse is often placed on hydraulic stilts. Thus the bargee can lift his cabin high enough to line up the vessel so it will pass safely between the sides of the arches, and then drop it down again so it will pass safely under the curve of the arch.

Just to impress the onlookers who are gawping from the bridges, the helmsmen leave their descent until the last moment. It's fun to watch.

Motorised Poop Scoops

There must be more dogs per head of population in Paris than in any other city in the world. The average Parisian, however, does not have a garden and this, as you can imagine, presents a problem. Paris pavements are notorious for "poop perils", as unwary pedestrians soon discover, and the authorities have been waging a campaign against the dreaded droppings. They put up thousands of billboards showing cartoon dogs with arrows directing droppings to the gutter. Alas, very few dogs can read and this strategy was not really effective.

Now they are trying something different. They have pioneered the Green Motorised Poop Scoop. The scoop is towed along behind a motorcycle. It is designed so it can be tugged up onto the pavement to scoop the poop. There are fifty of these machines at work. It's too soon to tell how successful the campaign is, but if you see a Motorised Poop Scoop, it is worth a photograph.

III
THINGS TO DO

Finding Out What's On

Paris is a beehive of activity. There are always new exhibitions, sporting events and concerts. Hollywood blockbuster movies often open in Paris before they come to London.

Ring 720-88-98 for a recorded summary in English of the latest events. Or buy the weekly guide, *Pariscope*. It costs about 3 francs and gives you up-to-the-minute information about what's on. Even if you don't read much French, you will be able to find your way around the magazine, and others like it.

When you see an American or British film marked with a "VO", that means it is in its *version originale* and it is not dubbed into French. Any film marked "VF" is in its *version française* and has been dubbed into French.

Parisians are keen on old comedy films. There is one cinema behind the Sorbonne that gives constant showings of Buster Keaton, Charlie Chaplin, the Marx Brothers, and all the other old-time Hollywood clowns. It is at 23 rue des Ecoles. Métro: Maubert Mutualité. See *Pariscope* for details.

Boat Trips

Be sure to plan a boat trip down the Seine and around the two islands. There are a great number of boats specially designed for river sightseeing. They make their trips throughout the day and into the night. The trip is really dramatic after dark when they use big floodlights. They are called *bateaux mouches* (bat-oh-moosh) which means "fly boats", because their glassed-in bodies make them look a bit like flies.

Boats leave regularly from the Pont d'Iena at the Eiffel Tower (Métro: Trocadéro, across the river and a little inconvenient), from the Pont d' Alma (Métro: Alma Marceau), and from the Pont Neuf on the Ile de la Cité (Métro: Pont Neuf).
The tours start from 10:30 am and at weekends and during peak seasons they run well into the evening.

Another boat trip is less glamorous but in its way just

as interesting. This is a cruise along the Canal St Martin, which is an old Parisian waterway. Leave yourself plenty of time for this one. The route takes you through some of the very old quarters of the city and runs underground to the Place de la Bastille.

It leaves across the square from the Métro Jean Jaurés. Departure time is 2 pm every day except Mondays. The trip is not made in the winter months.

Swimming

If the weather's warm, a session of open-air swimming might seem preferable to visiting a church or museum. The Piscine Deligny is open from May to September, and very popular too; it's on the Quai Anatole France 7e, at the edge of the river. There's the Piscine Molitor (which also has an indoor pool) at 8 avenue de la Porte-Molitor 16e; and the Piscine Georges Valleret, 148 avenue Gambetta 20e.

There are plenty of indoor pools too: see *Pariscope* under 'guide de Paris—piscines' for full details. A super modern pool in Henri de Montherlant, 32 boulevard de Montherlant, 16e. One more thing, for that very special occasion: if you're feeling particularly well-off, you can hire the Piscine de l'Etoile after 10 pm all to yourself for only 500 francs an hour.

On the subject of water, the Piscine Molitor also has an ice-skating rink; and there's another one, La Patinoire Gaîté Montparnasse, at 16 rue Vercingétorix 14e.

The Zoo

The biggest zoo in Paris is the Bois de Vincennes (bwuh-der-vah-sen). You're allowed to feed many of the animals there, but monkey nuts are expensive so it's better to take your own. Watching the baboons is really entertaining. They seem particularly playful and happy in their open-air enclosure. There's an interesting Incubation Room where you can see eggs hatch out and little chicks of all types being reared. It's housed at the foot of a concrete "mountain" that's over 200 feet high, which you can sometimes pay to climb up. The zoo also has a good variety of bears and big cats. A souvenir shop near the sea-lions sells miniature glass and china animals (10–15 francs) and close by is a café-restaurant that serves generous helpings of chicken and chips. If you've got a picnic, there's a lakeside nearby where you can sit and enjoy it, and boats are for hire, too.

The zoo is open daily from 9 am to 6 pm. It is closed one hour earlier in winter.
Métro: Porte Dorée.

IV
SHOPPING

Paris is great for shopping and better still for window-shopping. Everything from small souvenirs to diamond bracelets are presented with special flair and care. Even the plastic carrier-bags make good mementoes to take home.

Big stores usually stay open all day from 9:30 am to about 7 pm. Small shops generally take a long lunch break between 1 and 4 pm. Many of the food shops and markets are open on Sunday mornings. A lot of them are closed all day Monday.

The Big Stores

The best shopping areas for big stores are behind the Opéra on the Boulevard Haussmann, and on the rue de Rivoli between the Louvre and the Hôtel de Ville. Here are a few of the department stores, and a little bit about them.

La Samaritaine is one of the best all-round stores. It is on the rue de Rivoli and goes through to the Pont Neuf. (Métro: Pont Neuf). It is divided into shops called *Magasin* (mag-a-zah). Magasin no 4 is very good for stationery and brightly-coloured bags and satchels made of leather, canvas and plastic. There are games in this department too, and you can buy a set of *boules*. The basement of the main store has good china, and a delicatessen for food. There is a self-service restaurant on the roof. It has an excellent view.

Galeries Lafayette is very famous and very, very big. It is at 40, Boulevard Haussman. (Métro: Ch. Dantin). Good clothes, but rather expensive.

Le Printemps is just down the road from Galeries Lafayette. It has a department where you can buy unusual novelty candles. There is a roof café on the ninth floor.

BHV are the initials of Bazar de l'Hôtel de Ville. This big store is on the rue de Rivoli, just behind the Town Hall itself. (Métro: Hôtel de Ville). The stalls outside sell cheap bargains. There is also a place where they do engraving while you wait. Inside, the basement has a superb household department. (Wouldn't you fancy some Mickey Mouse taps for your bath?) The toy department is very good and has a lot of video and electronic games. Competitive prices.

Monoprix and Prisunic are two chains you will find scattered all over Paris. Their prices are low to moderate. Many of the smaller items are well within pocket-money range. They have a cheap, cheerful line in clothing, stationery and houseware. Some of their stores sell food.

Shopping Suggestions

Souvenirs: Some of the best souvenir shops are around Notre-Dame. Most of the big sights are good places to buy traditional mementoes, like models of the Eiffel Tower, or dolls dressed as French sailors. Don't forget the Musée de l'Affiche for posters, and the stalls along the Quais for antique postcards and maps.

Food: A tin of paté, a jar of Dijon mustard, or a packet of ground coffee make excellent gifts for friends and relatives. They are cheaper and generally more delicious than their English equivalents.

Stationery: A French diary has novelty value. There is good notepaper with tissue-lined envelopes, too. Notebooks, ringbinders, pens and ball-points are all that little bit different from anything you can buy at home.

Games: You can find Monopoly using French street names and telling you to *Allez directement au prison*. Metal sets of *boules* cost more than £30, but there are perfectly fine plastic and wooden ones around. Make sure the set you buy includes the little ball to aim at. It is called *le cochon* (le-coh-shon—the pig). If you choose a wooden set, check that there are no cracks.

Clothes: Parisians dress very well. They achieve their *chic* not so much by big items such as coats and dresses, but by choosing carefully their belts, scarves, jewellery, handbags and gloves. These are all on sale in big stores and often at bargain prices on stalls outside.

You can find cheap knitted hats or silk-style scarves with unmistakable French flair at Monoprix and Prisunic.

Plastic costume jewellery and hair-slides are made with originality and won't break your bank.

The trendiest boutiques are near the Pompidou Centre. Some of them sell 1950s secondhand clothes. Prices here range from reasonable to ridiculous.

If you are determined to make yourself bankrupt, head straight for the shops in the rue Faubourg St Honoré. The prices there are good for a laugh. Keep your eyes peeled for the word *Solde*. It means Sale.

Glassware and China: You can find coffee mugs with French slogans on them in the big stores, and wine glasses with green stems which are traditional for white wine, and very French. In the basement of *La Samaritaine* look out for *la poubelle de table* (poo-bell-der-tarble). This is a table waste-bin designed for putting chicken bones, fishbones, fruit pips and such into while you are eating at table.

Records: Nothing brings a holiday back to your mind better than a song you heard while you were away. The best all-round record shop is FNAC (fer-nack) in the Forum des Halles. (Métro: Les Halles). Some of the assistants speak English and can advise you on traditional French music, or hit pop songs.

There are bargain record shops along the Boulevard St Michel, near the river. (Métro: St Michel).

Paris Musique (pair-ee-moo-zeek) at No 10 Boulevard St Michel is particularly good for rock.

The French are big fans of jazz and if you are too, head for Le Monde du Jazz at 2, rue de la Petite Truanderie (Métro: Etienne Marcel).

Records are by and large more expensive in Paris, so don't bother buying anything you can find at home.

Junk: Antique shops in Paris are fabulously expensive. However, there are some markets selling second-hand or really old "treasures". The most famous of these is the Marché aux Puces (marsh-ay-oh-pooce), or Flea Market. It is a goodish walk from the Porte de Clignancourt Métro. Go on Saturday, Sunday or Monday morning, as early as you like. The market is open until lunchtime. You will find hundreds and hundreds of stalls selling crockery, old clothes, used spectacles, books, records, and also overpriced, rip-off rubbish. The market is worth seeing, and you never know your luck: you *might* find a bargain.

You have a better chance of discovering a real snip at one of the smaller flea markets not so popular with tourists. On Saturday and Sunday mornings there is one at Porte de Montreuil, another at the Porte de la Villette (in the rue du Chemin-de-fer), and yet another at the Place d'Aligre (Métro: Ledru-Rollin).

V
FOOD AND DRINK

Restaurants and Cafés

Adults often say there are only two countries in the world where the people understand food, and these are France and China. There are many tourists who go to France simply to eat. There are businessmen who will fly over to Paris just to have dinner. It will take you a little time to find your way around the amazing variety of Parisian food and drink. Here we give a few guidelines.

Breakfast (*Petit déjeuner*—p'tee-day-joo-nay). It is a casual business. Usually it is just bread and butter or flaky pastries called *croissants* (kwa-son) and big cups of milky coffee.

Cafés are as frequent in Paris as pubs in London. If your hotel does not serve breakfast, you can take it in a café, but it will be very expensive. The Parisians use their cafés all day long for drinks and small cups of thick, black coffee. There is no age limit, and unlike most pubs, cafés are brightly lit with big windows out on the street. To sip a drink while watching the world walk by is a favourite activity in Paris. Drinks cost more if you sit at a table but you can stay as long as you like, even if you buy just one thing. In the summer, many cafés have their tables out on the pavement. Here are a few café treats you might like to try.

Un citron pressé (ern-see-tron-press-ay) is freshly squeezed lemon juice served with a carafe of water and a bowl of sugar so you can make it to your own taste. Delicious on a hot day.

Un menthe à l'eau (ern-mon-ta-low) is a sweet peppermint syrup diluted with water. It is a gorgeous green colour and tastes like excellent tooth-paste.

Un diabolo menthe (ern-dee-ab-oh-low-mont) is mint with fizzy lemonade and tastes like even better toothpaste.

Un lait fraise (ern-lay-frezz) is cold milk and strawberry syrup. Delicious.

Un lait grenadine (ern-lay-grenn-a-deen) is milk and pomegranate syrup. Even more delicious.

Un éxpress (ern-es-press) is jitteringly strong black coffee in a small cup.

Un grand crème (ern-gron-krem) is frothy, milky coffee.

Un chocolat chaud (ern-shock-oh-la-show) is wonderful, frothy hot chocolate.

Un coca (ern-ko-ka) is what Parisians call a "coca cola". It is served with ice unless you say *pas de glace* (pa-der-glas).

Un sandwich (ern-sondweech) is a sandwich, generally made on a big chunk of crusty loaf. It can be *au fromage* (oh-from-arj) which means of cheese, *au jambon* (oh-zjom-bon) of ham, *au paté* (oh-pat-ay) of meat paste, *au saucisson sec* (oh-so-cease-on-seck) of chewy salami and garlic, *aux rillettes* (oh-ree-yet) of smokey pork brawn. *Un croque monsieur* (ern-crock-m'syer) is a toasted sandwich of ham and cheese, and *un croque madame* is the same thing but without the ham. *Un hot dog* (ern-ot-dog) is a frankfurter sausage stuffed into a small, crusty French loaf.

Lunch (déjeuner) and **dinner** (dîner) are the important meals in Paris. They are usually three courses washed down with wine. The French have lunch around 1 pm and wouldn't dream of having dinner before 7 pm. They eat out a lot more than the British do. Whole families often are seen dining at their local, inexpensive restaurant. Here are a few clues to the language of a Parisian menu.

Hors d'oeuvres (or-der-vrer) are starters. They are always served with fresh bread. There is no charge for bread. Ask for more if you need it.

Soupe a l'oignon (soop-a-loin-yon) is dark brown onion soup, sometimes under a crust of grilled cheese.
Oeuf dur mayonnaise (erf-dewr-may-on-ezz) are hard-boiled eggs with home-made mayonnaise.
Crudités (krood-ee-tay) are all sorts of raw vegetables grated or cut, served with a sharpish dressing of oil, vinegar and mustard.
Terrine (tear-een) is potted meat, sometimes of wild boar.
Champignons à la grecque (shomp-een-yon-à-la-grek) are cold, lightly-cooked mushrooms in a tart dressing.
Tête de veau (tet-der-voh) is jellied calf's head. An acquired taste. The French love it.

Cuisses de grenouilles (kweece-der-grun-wee) are frogs' legs. They taste a bit like chicken and are in a rich, garlic sauce.

Les Escargots (laze-ess-car-go) are snails. They taste like rubber bands in garlic. Generally, the snails are cooked out of their shells, then popped back in again. You will be given special tongs for holding the shells. These are not garden-variety snails, but specially raised on tender herbs. Actually, they're not bad.

Entrées or *Plats* (on-tray or plah) are main courses. Here are some for you.

Boeuf bourgignon (berf-boor-gee-nyon) is a dark beef stew made with red wine. Filling and good.

Cotelettes de veau (cut-er-let-der-voh) are grilled or fried veal cutlets. The French love their veal, which is tender and toothsome. *Côtelettes d'agneau* (cot-er-let-dan-yo) are lamb chops.

Coq au vin (cock-oh-van) is a chicken stew.

Cassoulet (kass-oo-lay) is a stew of beans with pork and mutton. A winter food.

Lapin chasseur (lap-an-shass-er) is rabbit cooked with wine and herbs. Very tasty.

Poulet rôti (poo-lay-row-tee) is roast chicken and generally served with chips.

Bifteck (biff-teck) is beefsteak and also served with chips. You order it "*saignant*" (sen-yon) for rare, *à point* (a-poo-an) for medium, and *bien cuit* (bee-en-coo-ee) for well-done. If you ask for it *bleu* (bler) it will be practically raw.

Poisson (pwass-on) means fish. The favourites are *truite* (tweet) or trout, *sole* (sol) or sole, *turbot* (toor-bow) or turbot. There are also varieties of shellfish which Parisians adore, especially *moules* (mool) or mussels, and *huîtres* (wee-truh) which are oysters.

Légumes (lay-goom) are vegetables. Generally you order them independently of your meat or fish. You can have *pommes frites* (pom-freet), possibly the best chips in the world, with *haricots verts* (arry-coh-vair) which are green beans, or *petits pois* (pity-pwah) which are sweet, tiny peas. You might try *ratatouille* (rat-at-too-ee), a spicy vegetable stew served hot or cold. Sensational.

Fromages (fro-mahje) means cheese and in Paris it is eaten as a separate course before the sweet. The French make too many cheeses to list here but the waiter will probably bring you *le plateau de fromage* (ler-pla-toe-der-fro-marj). This is a platter of many cheeses from which you can make your choice according to sight and smell.

Déserts (dezz-air) are sweets. They are mouth-watering and the portions are never too big.

Mousse au chocolat (moos-oh-sho-koh-lah) is a creamy, darkly chocolate custard which is good with *chantilly* (shan-tee-yee)—whipped cream.
Crème caramel (krem-car-ah-mel) is cream caramel. The French make the best in the world. They invented it.
Un mystère (ern-mist-air) means "a mystery". It is honey and hazelnut-coated ice cream. The mystery is how the cook gets the ball of meringue into the middle.
Tarte aux pommes (tar-toe-pom) is an apple tart. The French make it open and glazed on flaky pastry. There are all sorts of *tartes*, depending upon the fruit in season.

Boissons (bwah-son) mean drinks. Parisian children can be seen drinking wine with their meals, but it is generally very watered. You might try *eau minerale* (owe-min-er-al), mineral water, or just *eau naturelle* (owe-nat-er-all) which is still-water. There is always *un coca* or *un limonade* (ern-lim-on-ahd) which is fizzy lemonade.

Algeria was part of France until 1962, and many North Africans live in Paris. You will find lots of restaurants where you can eat their traditional cooking. *Cous-cous* is the most interesting and delicious of the North African dishes. It's a meal in itself of soup, meat, chicken and a hot sauce served separately. Its base is semolina grain, which is a bit like a tasty version of rice.

The Vietnamese also came to live in Paris. Vietnamese cooking is delicate and not too heavy. Definitely worth a try.

Self-service restaurants have become more and more popular, particularly with office-workers at lunchtime. They are quick and cheap. If you are doing a lot of walking and you value your time for sightseeing, you might want to lunch at a "self". A good one is on the fifth floor of "La Samaritaine" department store. It has a splendid view. It is best to go to a self-service before 12:30 when the ravenous hordes descend.

Picnics

When the weather is fine, persuade your party to take a picnic lunch to one of the parks, or to the riverside. Paris is full of places to buy perfect picnic food. There are lots of open markets, and supermarkets too for those who would rather not risk speaking French.

Every quarter of Paris has its own specialist shops. There is the *charcuterie* (shar-coot-ree) for cold-cuts, the *épicerie* (ay-pee-sree) for drinks, biscuits, tinned fish and, sometimes, fresh fruit. For cheese, you go to a *crèmerie* (krem-ree) or *fromagerie* (fro-mahj-ree). For bread, you go to a *boulangerie* (bool-on-jeree). The best picnic loaf is called a *baguette* (bag-ett), which means a stick or wand. You might prefer the thinner more crusty version called *une ficelle* (oon-fee-sell—a string). The fatter version is called *un grand pain* (ern-gron-pah). At the *patisserie* (pat-eece-ree) you can buy fanciful and delectable pastries.

If you do decide on a picnic, it's a good idea to wash fruit in fresh, running water, or even to peel it. There are lots of litter bins around. Please use them. Otherwise, you give us all a bad name.

On the hoof

If you want to eat on your feet, Paris is full of walk-about food. You might try wafer-thin pancakes called *crêpes* (crep) sold from stalls and dusted with sugar, or smeared with jam. In the winter, you'll want *marrons* (mah-rong) chestnuts sold hot from street-corner barrows. Many of the bakers sell individual little quiches, and slices of pizza. For the best of open-air snacks, just follow your nose.

The Parisians are also undergoing the Great Hamburger Invasion. You'll find them everywhere. They are all pretty much of a muchness.

The most famous of the many ice-cream places is Berthillon's on the Ile St Louis. They have all the usual flavours as well as more exotic treats such as Honey, Nougat, Kiwifruit, Rhubarb and Ginger, Pear, Wild Strawberry, and many more. The wonderful aroma in the street outside will tell you which is their special flavour of the day.

EMERGENCY

The only emergency you're likely to have to cope with on your own is getting lost. You can avoid this by *fixing somewhere to meet* when you go to crowded places like big stores or markets, in case you get separated. Fix on a particular stall or street corner and stay there at the pre-arranged time, don't wander away.

If all this fails, go back to your hotel. Always have

a little money and a Métro ticket with you and *note down your hotel address and telephone number* as soon as you know it. Fill it in at the bottom of this page. Find out the nearest Métro station and learn where it is on the map after you've arrived. If you do this you should have no trouble getting back, but if you're still stuck show the form at the bottom of this page to a policeman.

In an ABSOLUTE EMERGENCY you can contact the American Embassy at:

**2, Avenue Gabriel,
75008 Paris
Telephone: 296 12 02 261**

Fill this out as soon as you have the information:

AU SECOURS

(Name)	**Je m'appelle:**
(Hotel)	**J'habite:**
(Address)	**L'adresse:**
(tel. no)	**No. de tel:**

Index

Antiques 81
Arènes de Lutèce 7, 53
Armistice Day 14
arrondissements 14, 16
art nouveau 17
au secours 91
Austerlitz, Battle of 41
Avenue President Wilson 25, 57

Bastille 9, 14, 41
bateaux mouches 74
Bazar de l'Hotel de Ville (B.H.V.) 78
Beaubourg (see Pompidou Centre)
boules 12, 45, 67
Boulevard de Palais 38
Boulevard Haussmann 77
Boulevard St. Germain 45
Boulevard St. Michel 45, 81
Braille, Louis 54
burecux de change 24

Canal St. Martin 75
un carnet 20
Champs Elysées 8, 11, 36
Charles VII 8
Chopin 44
Cimitière de Montmartre 40
Clothes 80
Comédie-Française 48
concierge 12
Concorde Bridge 41
Corday, Charlotte 49
"la Coupole" 62
Crown of Thorns 37

Danton 41
de Gaulle, Charles 11, 13, 35, 36
Dinner 85
Duels 47
Duke of Wellington 10

Ecole Militaire 29
Egyptian Obelisk 41
Eiffel Tower 10, 23, **28**, 74, 79
Elysée Palace 13
Emergency **90**
Etoile 36

fiacre 64
First World War 11, 36, 43, 65
Fitzgerald, F. Scott 62
Flea Market 81, 82
Forum des Halles 80
Franc 23
Freedom Fighters 46, 49

Galeries Lafayette 78
Games 79
Gauguin 39
Germany 10, 11, 43, 49, 63
Glassware and China 80
Gothic 29, 30, 37
Grand Palais 55
Doctor Guillotin 9
Guillotine 9, 41, 50, 63

Les Halles 70
Henry VI 8
Hitler 36
Hugo, Victor 47, 54
Hunchback of Notre-Dame 31, 47

Ice Cream 90
Ice-Skating Rink 75
Ile de la Cité 7, 16, 48, 74
Ile St. Louis 16, 90
Impressionism 39
Impressionists 38, 39

Jardin d'Acclimatation 58, 59
Joan of Arc 8
Julius Caesar 7
Junk 81

The Lady and the Unicorn 44
Left Bank 7, 16, 67
Lenin 62
Leonardo da Vinci 32
Louis XIII 48
Louis XIV (The Sun King) 8, 68, 69
Louis XVI 8, 9, 41
Louis-Philippe 45
Louvre 7, 8, **32**, 45, 77
Lumière, Auguste and Louis 64
Lunch 85
Luxembourg Palace 13, 67

Madame Tussaud   63
la Madeleine, Church of   41
Maine-Montparnasse Tower   62
Manet   39
Le Marais   47, 60
Marat, Jean-Paul   49
Marché aux Puces   81, 82
Marie-Antoinette   41, 51, 58, 68
Mayor of Paris   14
Michelangelo   33
Miniature Railway   58
Modigliani   39
Mona Lisa   32, 33
Monet   39
Monoprix   26, 78
Montmartre   **39**, 51
Montparnasse   **62**
Motorised Poop Scoops   **72**
Moulin Rouge   51
Mucha, Alfons   51
Musée de Montmartre   40
Musée National des Arts et Traditions Populaires   59
Museum of French Monuments   64

Napoleon Bonaparte   9, 13, 29, 32, 36, 42, 43
Napoleon III   10, 61
National Assembly   13, 41
National Folk Museum   59
Natural History Museum   53
Notre-Dame Cathedral   7, 10, 25, **29**, 30, 78

Palais Bourbon   13
Palais de Chaillot   56, 60, 64, 66
Palais Galliéra   57
Palais de Justice   38
Palais de Luxembourg   13, 67
Palais de Tokyo   65
Paris Commune   10, 45, 63
Pariscope   73
Parisii   7
Parliament   13
Picasso   62
Pickpockets   21
Piscine Deligny   75
Piscine Molitor   75
Pissaro   39
Place de la Concorde   13, 23, 39, **41**, 45, 69
Place du Tertre   40

Planetarium   55, 56
Pompidou, Georges   11, 35
Pont d'Alma   50, 74
Pont d'Iena   74
Pont Neuf   74, 77
Porte Maillot   58, 59
Postcards   25, 26
President   11, 13
le Printemps   78
Prisunic   26, 78

Records   80
Renoir   39
Resistance   49
Restaurants   83
Revolution   9, 13, 54, 57, 63, 64, 65
Richelieu, Cardinal   48
Right Bank   16, 48
Robespierre   41
Rodin, Auguste   52
Romans   7, 44, 49, 53
Rousseau   54
Rue Faubourg St. Honoré   13, 80
Rue de la Paix   10
Rue de Rivoli   10, 26, 44, 45, 78

Sacré-Coeur   10, 39
La Samaritaine   77, 80, 88
Sartre, Jean-Paul   62
Second World War   11, 14, 46, 62
Seine, River   7, 16, 25, 41, 47, 71, 74
Senate   13, 67
Seurat   39
Snacks   90
solde (sale)   80
Sorbonne University   16, 74
Stationery   79
Stravinsky   62

tarif reduit   28
têtes de station   22
"The Thinker"   52
Toulouse Lautrec   39, 51

Van Gogh   39
Venus de Milo   33
Versailles   8
Voltaire   54

Waterloo, Battle of   10, 13, 42
Waxworks   63

Zola, Emile   54

93